SPORTS HEROES AND LEGENDS

Wilma
Rudolph

Read all of the books in this exciting, action-packed biography series!

Hank Aaron

Muhammad Ali

Lance Armstrong

Barry Bonds

Roberto Clemente

Joe DiMaggio

Tim Duncan

Dale Earnhardt Jr.

Lou Gehrig

Mia Hamm

Tony Hawk

Derek Jeter

Michael Jordan

Sandy Koufax

Michelle Kwan

Mickey Mantle

Shaquille O'Neal

Jesse Owens

Jackie Robinson

Alex Rodriguez

Wilma Rudolph

Babe Ruth

Ichiro Suzuki

Tiger Woods

SPORTS HEROES AND LEGENDS

Wilma Rudolph

by Tom Streissguth

BARNES & NOBLE
NEW YORK

Contents

Three Gold Medals

A tall, slender African American woman stood quietly in place, listening for the sound of a gun. Wilma Rudolph was just 100 meters (330 feet) from her goal, poised on a long asphalt running track marked with white chalk.

The crowd above and around her murmured with excitement. Wilma's three teammates in the race, the women's 4x100-meter relay, took their positions and silently waited. Their competitors, relay teams from six other countries, listened for the gun as well.

Wilma was standing in the center of the Olympic Stadium, on the outskirts of Rome, Italy. It was September 1960, and she was competing in her second Olympic Games. She had already won two gold medals in these games. A win in the 4x100 relay would give the Tennessee native a third gold medal and a perfect record.

Wilma knew her teammates well. They were all Tigerbelles, champion student athletes from Tennessee State University in Nashville. In this group of elite runners, Wilma ran the anchor, or final, leg of the relays, the spot reserved for the fastest woman on the team.

The judges, the timekeeper, and the crowd watched the runners. The starter gave his commands in Italian: "On your mark!" and "Ready!" The starting gun fired.

Wilma waited and watched as her teammates—Martha Hudson, Barbara Jones, and Lucinda Williams—sped around the track one after another. As each runner finished her 100-meter lap, she handed off a stick called a baton to the next runner on the team.

Then it was Wilma's turn to run. Lucinda Williams, the third-leg runner, sprinted toward her. Wilma began running as Lucinda approached, her eyes intent on the baton, her hand extended. Lucinda drew up behind Wilma, the baton moving quickly with the motion of her arm. Wilma reached out, but she couldn't get a good grip. She slowed, stopped to grab the baton, then took off again.

During the bobbled handoff, Germany's Jutta Heine had passed Wilma and taken the lead. But Wilma turned on the speed and was soon running with Heine. Both runners strained to hit the tape. By a split second, Wilma Rudolph came in first.

She had won another gold medal, becoming the first American woman ever to win three gold medals at the Olympic Games.

Wilma Rudolph was just twenty years old. Her legs were slender, their muscles strong. But not long before, Wilma had had trouble walking and even standing straight. A childhood illness had disabled her. For many years, she had had to walk with a metal brace on her leg. But hard work and patience and the love and attention of her family eventually allowed her to walk normally. She exceeded expectations by playing basketball, running track, and becoming an Olympic champion.

As she stood on the medal stand after the victory, Wilma Rudolph savored the moment. Her years of hardship and hard work had finally paid off in a big way. Reporters, fans, and spectators all over the globe knew who she was: the fastest woman in the world.

Chapter One

Struggling at the Start

In the town of Saint Bethlehem, Tennessee, Wilma Rudolph was born to Ed and Blanche Rudolph on June 23, 1940. She arrived eight weeks prematurely (before her due date), weighing only 4.5 pounds and struggling to breathe. Many times in the first few months of Wilma's life, Blanche Rudolph wondered whether her daughter would even survive.

Soon after Wilma's birth, her parents moved to the nearby city of Clarksville. They rented a red, wood-frame house on Kellogg Street, in Clarksville's African American neighborhood. On this street, the houses had no electricity, no central heating, and no indoor plumbing. The Rudolphs went to the bathroom in an outhouse. They burned kerosene lamps to light their home in the evening.

In the 1940s, when Wilma was growing up, Clarksville was segregated. Segregation meant that by law and custom, blacks and whites stayed apart, as they did in many other cities in the southern United States. White and black children attended different schools. Certain stores were open to whites only, while others served blacks. Because they held positions of power in business and government, whites attended the better schools, lived in the better neighborhoods, and held the better-paying jobs. In Clarksville, everyone in town accepted segregation as a fact of life, and every African American family faced its sting every day.

The town of Saint Bethlehem, where Wilma Rudolph was born, has disappeared. In the 1980s, the city of Clarksville officially took Saint Bethlehem into its city limits. After that, Saint Bethlehem was just another Clarksville neighborhood.

The Rudolph clan was huge. Wilma was the sixth child born to Ed and Blanche Rudolph. Ed Rudolph also had fourteen children from a previous marriage. Two more children would be born after Wilma, making the Rudolphs a family of twenty-two children in all. By the time Wilma was born, many of her older siblings had grown up and moved away. But everyone in the family was close. Her older brothers, sisters, half brothers, and half sisters often came to visit. Christmas was a happy and crazy time, when the entire family came home to Kellogg Street for a big holiday meal.

Ed Rudolph worked as a railroad porter. Porters, who were nearly all African Americans, worked on passenger trains, taking care of overnight travelers during long journeys. The job demanded long hours. While on the job, Ed had to leave the family for days and sometimes weeks at a time. His pay was low. To earn extra money, Ed also worked as a handyman in Clarksville. Blanche Rudolph did cooking, laundry, and house-cleaning for wealthy white families in town. "The way my mother worked," Wilma later wrote, "somebody should have been serving *her* coffee in bed on Saturday mornings."

Wilma's parents both worked hard, managing to keep a household together without any outside help. They were religious people, attending a Baptist church every Sunday. Around the house, Ed Rudolph was very strict. He didn't stand for any misbehavior. The children feared his temper. Many years later, Wilma remembered how the house grew quiet and still whenever her father arrived home from work.

Ed and Blanche had to take special care of Wilma, who was underweight and suffered one illness after another. At age four, she came down with double pneumonia and scarlet fever. She also caught measles, mumps, and chicken pox. For long periods, she felt too sick to get out of bed. Wilma eventually recovered from all these illnesses. But the worst of them, the one that stayed with her, was polio.

POLIO

Poliomyelitis, or polio, is a disease caused by a virus. In most cases, the polio virus stays in a person's digestive system and causes no symptoms at all. In some mild cases, it feels like the flu or a bad cold, or it causes sore muscles in the back or neck. But in a few cases, the virus enters the bloodstream. It attacks the nerves controlling the muscles of the arms, legs, and other parts of the body. Some victims are unable to stand or walk.

A doctor named Jonas Salk developed a polio vaccine (a drug that prevents the illness) in 1955. Doctors gave the vaccine to children throughout the United States and many other countries. By the twenty-first century, polio had almost disappeared from the world.

Polio was a dreaded illness when Wilma was growing up. In many cases, polio brings mild symptoms, no worse than the flu. But Wilma had the bad kind of polio, the kind that can leave a victim permanently disabled. In her case, the polio weakened her left leg. As the illness grew worse, she couldn't walk or even stand. She had to spend her days in bed or sitting in a living-room chair. Worse, the local elementary school wouldn't allow her to enroll until she could walk. While her siblings and neighborhood kids headed off to school every morning, Wilma had to stay home in a silent, boring house.

66*Being left behind had a terrible effect on me. I was so lonely, and I felt rejected. . . . I cried a lot.*99

—WILMA RUDOLPH

Her mother had patiently nursed her through her many sicknesses. But for the polio, Wilma's mother needed good medical help and advice. Dr. Coleman, one of the only African American doctors in town, believed that Wilma would never walk or run normally. Blanche Rudolph wouldn't listen to that opinion. She wouldn't give up on her daughter.

Clarksville Memorial Hospital, on Madison Street, was for whites only—Wilma couldn't pass through its doors. And the Home Infirmary, Clarksville's hospital for African Americans, didn't treat polio patients. So one day, Wilma and her mother traveled by bus to Nashville, almost fifty miles from Clarksville, to the Meharry Medical College, a hospital for African Americans. There, Mrs. Rudolph talked to several doctors about Wilma's condition. She learned that there was no drug to cure polio. The doctors and the clinic could offer her only advice and encouragement. They recommended regular sessions of physical therapy, massage, and hot whirlpool baths to help Wilma's leg. They also fitted Wilma with a steel leg brace, attached to a heavy brown shoe. The brace and shoe were supposed to keep her leg straight.

Every week, Wilma and Blanche took the bus to Nashville. Wilma enjoyed these outings. She loved looking out the bus window at the trees, hills, and farms along the route. "I was getting out of Clarksville," she remembered. "I was seeing other things. I was traveling."

But there was one aspect of the trip that Wilma did not enjoy. Like other public facilities, bus stations were segregated in the late 1940s. Wilma recalled the bus station in Clarksville: "It had a black ticket window, a black waiting area, a black bathroom. [If you] were black, and you went to the bus station, you didn't even get near the white people who were making the same trip. When you got to Nashville, you might be hungry but too bad. There was this little restaurant in the Nashville bus station, and it was for whites only. You were black, you had to find someplace else to eat. . . . That was the way it was in the South back then."

Mrs. Rudolph was a working woman, and she didn't have time to take her daughter to Meharry for regular therapy sessions. So she had the doctors there show her how to massage Wilma's leg. Every evening, after returning from her job, she would set to work. She would run her strong hands up and down Wilma's leg, trying to get the muscles working and the blood circulating. She also wrapped the leg in hot towels and made Wilma lie underneath heavy blankets to sweat out the sickness.

After a year of home treatment, Wilma showed only a little improvement. But Mrs. Rudolph was a determined woman. She was certain that Wilma would run and walk normally, and she didn't give up easily. She sat with Wilma for as long as she could, massaging her leg. She taught three older children how to do the massage as well.

❝ *My doctors told me I would never walk again. My mother told me I would. I believed my mother.* **❞**

—WILMA RUDOLPH

Wilma, in the meantime, was left out of the fun that took place just outside her front door. She spent many long afternoons watching from a window as the other kids played. Sometimes, she did venture outside, struggling with her leg and her brace. Neighborhood kids often teased her about her leg

10

and called her names. But her older brothers and sisters always stuck up for her.

As her leg strengthened, Wilma learned to stand and to take short hops around the house. As often as not, the leg would give out, and she would tumble to the floor. But her mother set a good example—she didn't give up. She told her daughter that someday she would walk and run as well as anyone.

Chapter Two

Little Fighter

L iving with a disability was tough. But Wilma faced an even tougher problem in Clarksville. Even as a little girl, she could see that white people looked down on her. Whenever she went to a grocery store with friends, the white owner would look them over suspiciously. If they talked too loudly or grew a little boisterous, the owner would run them out into the street. If Wilma's family wanted to eat out, they had to go to Lander's Café, the only restaurant in town that would serve African Americans.

Once Wilma sat with a group of friends on a grassy hill overlooking the Montgomery County Fair. The children could not afford to buy fair tickets. As they sat and watched, Wilma saw exhibitors carefully grooming and walking their beloved horses. The thought came to Wilma: White people treat their animals better than they treat us.

Wilma began to ask her parents questions. Why did all the African Americans in town live apart, eat in a different place, and go to school only with their own kind? Blanche and Ed told her not to worry about it. That's the way things were in Clarksville, they said, and there was nothing she could do about it.

WILMA'S HOMETOWN

Clarksville was founded near the Kentucky border in 1785 and named for George Rogers Clark, a frontiersman, Revolutionary War hero, and older brother of William Clark, a famous western explorer. Clarksville has a long history. Its newspaper, the *Leaf-Chronicle*, is the oldest newspaper in Tennessee.

Wilma grew angry. She began to think that all white people were mean and evil. She wanted nothing to do with them. She also felt determined to break out of this segregated world somehow. Contrary to what her parents said, she felt there was something she could do—or some other place she could go. A place had to exist where people wouldn't notice the color of her skin.

At the age of seven, Wilma began her schooling at Cobb Elementary, where all the kids were African American. At first she was frightened. She had spent a lot of time in her house, sitting alone, and had never socialized with strangers. But soon the other kids accepted her. Her leg was growing stronger. Despite the brace, she played outside every day with friends and schoolmates.

When she was eight, doctors fitted Wilma with a new, high-top left shoe. With the brace and the new shoe, she could walk around the neighborhood and manage the eight blocks to school. But she didn't like the look or feel of the shoe. It was ugly, a mark of her disability. She waited impatiently for the day when she could leave it in the closet.

She didn't let the brace, the shoe, or her weak left leg prevent her from playing and competing with siblings and friends. She would sometimes take off the heavy shoe and play in her bare feet. When her parents weren't looking, she would also take off the leg brace and try to move around on her weak left leg. She had her siblings warn her at the approach of her mother or father so she could quickly put the brace back on. The secret walking helped strengthen her leg.

At the age of nine, Wilma walked for the first time without her leg brace. It happened at a Sunday church service. As her friends, family, and neighbors looked on, she walked up the church aisle and sat down in the pew without any help. The onlookers admired her new strength and ability.

When she was twelve years old, she decided she didn't need the brace at all. Her mother happily sent it back to the Meharry clinic in Nashville, a place they didn't need to go anymore. Soon afterward, the heavy shoe was also retired from service. Mrs. Rudolph came home with the best gift Wilma could have: a pair of shiny, and normal, black leather shoes.

After her mother returned the leg brace to Nashville, Wilma spent lots of time running around the backyard of her home in Clarksville. She shot hoops into a wooden peach basket set up in the yard. She dribbled basketballs across the dusty ground, keeping one eye on the basket, the other on her opponent.

OLD-FASHIONED BASKETBALL

Wilma and her brother Wesley loved playing basketball in their backyard. No stores sold portable basketball goals in the 1940s. Instead, any kid who wanted to shoot hoops simply punched out the bottom of a wooden peach basket and hung the basket on a pole. That was how basketball was first played, when Dr. James Naismith invented the game in Springfield, Massachusetts, in 1891.

With some neighborhood boys, Wilma and her brother Wesley formed competing teams. They played basketball for hours, in all kinds of weather. They were always up and out of bed early to go out back and play. When school was out, they played past sundown, until the wooden peach basket disappeared in the dusk. Blanche Rudolph sometimes watched from the house, worried that Wilma's leg would give out. But Wilma just kept playing and playing.

---

66 *Not one of all my boys ever played as hard as that child making up all the playing time she'd missed. I would watch her nearly about to cry.* 99

—BLANCHE RUDOLPH, WILMA'S MOTHER

One thing still held Wilma back. She was skinny. During basketball games, she couldn't push opponents away or get under the basket for a rebound. So she had to be quick and sly. By the rules the kids used, players kept to certain spots on the court, so Wilma didn't have to run very much. In a very short time, she had no problem scoring as often as her brothers and the neighborhood boys.

Wilma had spent many years sitting in the house. So after the brace came off, she made up for lost time. She couldn't stand to be inside anymore and spent every free hour outside. When dinnertime came, her mother sometimes had to chase her inside with a switch—a short, slender branch used to discipline children.

❝I was determined to find out what life held for me beyond the inner-city streets.❞

—WILMA RUDOLPH

The basketball games helped strengthen Wilma's leg. They helped her walk and run normally. The kids at school forgot that she had ever been different from them. She was no longer the skinny girl with the leg brace. Instead, she was the fastest kid on the basketball court.

She wanted to become an athlete, to compete on a real basketball court and to play for a coach and fans. But Cobb Elementary had no sports teams for her to join. In the seventh grade, she hoped, things would change. She would be going to a new school and starting a new life.

Chapter | Three

Running, Jumping, Winning

In seventh grade, Wilma began attending Burt High School, another all-African American school. The school combined junior and senior high grades. It was a new school, and most of the kids were excited and happy to be there. The school offered social clubs, after-school activities, and sports teams. Wilma's older sister Yvonne played on the girls' basketball squad. Wilma followed Yvonne's example and tried out for the team.

The coach, Clinton Gray, didn't think much of Wilma's abilities. He thought Yvonne was a better player and told Wilma she would have to wait a year or two before playing for Burt High. But when Ed Rudolph heard about the decision, he sent the coach a message: Either Wilma and Yvonne would join the team together or neither of them would.

The coach agreed, reluctantly, to accept Wilma. But he sat her on the bench and didn't put her in a single game her entire first year. Even so, Wilma was thrilled to be part of the team. She loved practice and enjoyed away games—games at other schools—that allowed her to travel. The team went by bus to other small towns in northern Tennessee and southern Kentucky. Getting away from Clarksville and seeing new places was always a treat.

DR. BURT

Wilma's high school was named after Dr. Robert Tecumseh Burt. The son of freed slaves, Dr. Burt had been born in Mississippi and had trained as a doctor at the Meharry Medical College in Nashville. He moved to Clarksville in 1902 and opened the town's first medical clinic for African American residents. In 1906 Dr. Burt set up the Home Infirmary, the first African American hospital in Clarksville. Dr. Burt managed the infirmary for forty-eight years.

Sitting on the bench, Wilma watched and patiently waited for her turn to play. When the team won, she celebrated. When they lost, she fretted. In the meantime, she studied everything that was happening: how the players passed, shot, rebounded, and drew fouls; how the referees kept control of the games. She also watched how the coach made substitutions and how the home crowds supported their teams with yells and cheers. Everything about basketball was exciting and fun.

In her eighth-grade year, Coach Gray put Wilma in a few games—always at the last minute, always with the Burt team way ahead. At the end of this year, Wilma had something else to look forward to: Coach Gray had started a track team. He asked all the girls on the basketball team if they wanted to join. Wilma didn't hesitate. Running would be fun, she thought, and it would give her something to do in the late afternoon. The last thing she wanted to do after school was trudge home.

LADYLIKE BASKETBALL

When Wilma Rudolph was playing for Burt High School, women's basketball was played differently from men's basketball. Women's teams had six players on a side, while men played with five on a side. Unlike the men's game, female players were restricted to a certain zone of play. Players could bounce the ball only twice and hold it for only three seconds before passing. The women's rules forced a lot of passing and prevented physical contact and fouls. Many people of the era thought that girls shouldn't be playing boys' games, so these rules made the game as "ladylike" as possible.

For Wilma, track practices were much easier than basketball workouts. She already had natural speed and determination. Every day, the coach had the team jog around a field for a while, then run some footraces. The girls formed a big pack at the starting line. The coach stood alone in the distance and gave the signal for everyone to run toward him. The first one to run past the coach was the winner—and Wilma won every time.

A few times, the coach told his team to sprint down lanes, the way runners did in a real competition. For these races, the coach taught Wilma the basics of starting. She had to dig a small hole in the ground with her foot and set her back foot against the hole for balance. She crouched down, her legs bent at the knees and her arms in front. Her hands rested on the ground to keep her balanced, but her weight stayed on her feet. Her head looked down the track without straining.

Good starts were important, Wilma learned. But there was a lot of strategy to running sprints (short-distance races). Wilma found that the more she learned about running, the more she needed to learn. The coach taught her many tricks to make her faster. She was a natural runner, and with practice she knew she could be the fastest girl in school.

In the year that followed, Wilma's basketball skills also improved. She had spent many years watching her friends and brothers play. She had already learned much just by watching. By ninth grade, fourteen-year-old Wilma was lightning quick and a dead-eye shooter.

Wilma took the game seriously, not like many students who played just for fun. The art of stealing the ball really got her attention. She learned to study her opponents while they dribbled the basketball, looking for an open shot or a chance to pass. Sometimes, their eye or body movements revealed where they were going to run or pass. They often lost their concentration just before passing. Wilma waited for that moment of inattention. When an opponent's eyes moved away from her, she lunged for the ball. With her quick hands, she often came up with a steal. She soon became an expert basketball thief.

"SKEETER"

Wilma's quick legs and reflexes caused problems for Coach Gray. Sometimes he had a hard time spotting her on the court, and sometimes he saw her everywhere. "You're buzzing around like a skeeter [mosquito] wherever I turn!" he once said in exasperation. From that time forward, Wilma's nickname was Skeeter.

Coach Gray may have noticed her skills, but during her ninth-grade year, he still didn't play her much. He saw her as young and inexperienced. He also thought she was too small and thin to match up with opponents. In practice, he let her play against his first-string players, but he rarely put her into games. Wilma rode the bus with the team and rode the bench during the game. She grew frustrated and angry. She knew she was getting faster and better, playing smart and practicing hard. But it didn't seem to matter to the coach.

In the spring of her ninth-grade year, Wilma went out for track again. The practices took place inside the school on cold days and outside when it was warm enough. For the coach, track was a way of keeping his basketball team in shape. For Wilma, track was becoming even more interesting than basketball. As a member of a track team, she ran for herself. She didn't have to wait for the coach to put her in a game. She could shine on her own, just by trying harder than the rest.

The area high schools in Clarksville had no running tracks. Meets were held outdoors, in open fields marked out with chalk lines. Wilma ran in five different events: the 50-, 75-, 100-, and 200-meter sprints and the relays, when four girls on a team ran 100 meters, one after another. She won every single race she entered. But winning was nothing special. The opponents weren't very good, and almost nobody came to the meets. Still, winning sprints and relays was a lot more fun than sitting on the bench in a basketball game.

Before tenth grade started, in the fall of 1955, Wilma decided to work even harder at basketball. Even before the season or regular practices began, she showed up at the gym to practice with her friend Nancy Bowen. The two dribbled, shot, and played one on one. They made sure that Coach Gray knew what they were doing. Wilma wanted the coach to see how serious she was about playing basketball. She thought she was good enough to play, and even start, for the Burt High girls' team.

Coach Gray didn't like to let on what he was thinking. But Wilma and Nancy knew they had a chance to become starters. With all the work they had put in, they *deserved* a chance. They worked and waited patiently for the coach to make up his mind about the starting lineup.

Finally, after many afternoons of preseason practice, the night of the first game arrived. At the last minute, the coach picked out his starters. He went up and down the bench, tugging on the sleeves of the players he wanted. Wilma's friend Nancy Bowen made it and so did Wilma—as a guard.

Through her sophomore year, Wilma started for the Burt High School girls' basketball team. In one game, she scored 32 points and didn't miss a shot or a free throw. That year, the team went 11 and 4, with all the losses to teams out of their own Middle East Tennessee Conference. Within the conference, Burt High shut out the competition—they didn't have a single loss. They easily won the conference title.

 Both of Wilma Rudolph's Clarksville schools—Cobb Elementary and Burt High School—no longer exist. They were torn down to make way for the Burt-Cobb Community Center, which stands on Franklin Street in Clarksville.

As the conference winner, Burt qualified for the state tournament, held at Pearl High in Nashville. In the first round of the tournament, Nancy Bowen led the team with 30 points. Wilma sank most of her shots and free throws to score 26. Burt easily won that game. But in the second round, the team played badly and got beat.

The tournament loss was a disappointment. The season was suddenly over, and not in a good way. Wilma had played well, but basketball was a team game. Winning or losing came down to which group of teammates played best together. The Burt High team hadn't been the best.

Even though Burt lost, Wilma had drawn attention with her quick moves and her ability to score, dribble, and steal. One of the conference referees, Ed Temple, had officiated at several of her games and took notice of her. He saw that she had ability, but he also saw that she had her lazy moments—times when she was holding back and just seemed to be watching everybody else.

Ed Temple was a leader in both sports and academics. While creating and guiding the powerhouse women's track team at Tennessee State University (TSU), Temple also worked at TSU as a professor of sociology.

Wilma didn't know it yet, but Ed Temple was also a scout—someone who seeks out talented players for advanced-level teams. While working as a referee, he was searching for athletes for Tennessee State University (TSU), an all-African American college in Nashville. He worked there as both a teacher and a women's track coach. With Ed Temple's eye for athletic talent, TSU's women's track team had become one of the best track teams in the country. The men's teams at TSU were called the Tigers, so the women's track team was known as the Tigerbelles.

Watching her on the basketball court, Ed Temple thought that Wilma Rudolph might make a good addition to his track team. With her natural ability, tall and thin build, with long legs, he believed she could help take the Tennessee State Tigerbelles to national track meets—and win.

Chapter Four

Summer Tigerbelle

At first running track was just something for Wilma to do when basketball season was over. She wasn't too serious about it, and she trained without any real goals. Like many other girls on the Burt High track team, she had her mind on other things: schoolwork, her family, and socializing with her friends.

She also had a boy to think about. His name was Robert Eldridge. Robert and Wilma had known each other for a long time. When she was much younger and walking with a brace, he had been just another mean boy. He teased her and sometimes threw rocks at her when she passed on the street. As he got older, he started to change. Wilma noticed that Robert was at heart a good person. By the time she started high school, she was going out with Robert. Like the other girls who were dating, she sometimes wore his letterman's jacket around school.

In her sophomore year, after the basketball tournament in Nashville, Wilma started to get more serious about track. She was beating everyone at the meets. Her coach and teammates cheered her on and let her know how good she was. She would sometimes even cut classes to go out and practice running. This time, she was preparing for something big: an interstate meet on the campus of the Tuskegee Institute in southeastern Alabama.

The Tuskegee meet was the high point of the year for girls' track. African American high schools from all over the South sent their girls' teams to the meet. Wilma heard a lot of warnings about how good the other runners were going to be. She didn't worry about it, though. She knew that she was good and that she never lost.

Her confidence lasted up until her first race. At the finish line, for the very first time in her career, someone finished ahead of her. She lost that race and every other race at Tuskegee to far better runners from Atlanta.

In Alabama, Wilma learned an important lesson. She was good, but she wasn't good enough. Her natural talent would get her only so far. She needed work—and lots of it. She had to get much better at the mechanics of track: how to start, how to run, how to use her arms, how to hold her head, how to pace herself, and how to push at the finish line. Success in track required a lot more than just running fast. Wilma realized there was strategy involved, and the best runners knew how to use that strategy to win.

Meanwhile, TSU coach Ed Temple hadn't forgotten about Wilma Rudolph. Every year, Temple invited some high school athletes to a summer track camp at Tennessee State University. If they proved good enough, he arranged for them to attend TSU.

ANOTHER TSU CHAMPION

Tennessee State trained great male athletes as well as female athletes. A TSU long jumper, Ralph Boston, won the National Collegiate Athletic Association (NCAA) long-jump title in 1960. Later that year, he broke a twenty-four-year-old world record set by Jesse Owens at the 1936 Olympics in Berlin, Germany. Boston then went to the 1960 Olympics in Rome, where he won the gold. In later Olympics, he won silver and bronze medals.

In May 1956, Coach Temple traveled to Clarksville to invite Wilma to Tennessee State for his summer sports camp. He arrived at the Rudolph home on Kellogg Street to talk over the idea with Wilma's parents. He explained what the camp was all about and what Wilma would do there. Wilma, just fifteen years old, would train with both high school and college athletes. She would have a chance to race against good competition and learn the strategy of running. Temple also explained that the camp's gifted teenage athletes, if they finished high school, could win a scholarship (free tuition) to study at TSU. Wilma pleaded with her parents to let her attend the camp.

The Rudolphs liked what the coach had to say. They were most pleased about the chance for Wilma to get a college education. If she won a scholarship to TSU, she would be the first child in the family to attend college. They agreed to let her attend Temple's camp.

Coach Temple held practices at an oval dirt track on the outskirts of the Tennessee State campus. It was a rough and uneven track, with ruts and grooves pounded into the dirt—a far cry from the good cinder tracks used by colleges with more money to spend. Pebbles in the lanes could throw off a runner's stride, even twist an ankle if the runner came down on them the wrong way. In the hot summer months, the track could also smell pretty bad—one end of it nearly reached a local garbage dump.

Early that summer, Coach Temple drove Wilma to Nashville, then showed her to her dorm room in Wilson Hall. The team assigned Wilma a roommate, Martha Hudson, and the two runners settled in. At the first practice, an equipment man handed out uniforms: T-shirts, shorts, and sweat suits. But the coach had his runners wear heavy basketball shoes instead of lightweight track shoes. The heavy shoes served a purpose. The runners would use them for a while to build up the muscles in their legs before switching to track shoes.

"RUN LIKE CRAZY"

Coach Ed Temple wanted his TSU Tigerbelles to put forth a good image. He insisted on conservative dress and behavior at all times. The Tigerbelles were not allowed to wear flashy clothes. They were to avoid trouble around campus, not drive or ride in cars unless going to or from their homes, and go to bed early. They were to study hard and maintain a B average in class. Coach Temple's motto was "Act like a lady, but run like crazy."

Wilma found herself working hard alongside a lot of older girls. The routine was tough. Five days a week, they were up at dawn and running cross-country for six miles. After breakfast, they ran another six miles, and in the afternoon another six. The coach used these long jogs through the countryside to build up the runners' endurance.

The runs—over fields and dirt paths, across farms, to an oil-tank facility, and then back again—were brutal. Wilma ran hard to keep up with the others. She sometimes struggled and gasped for air. Slowly but surely, by keeping at it, she built up her lung power and muscle conditioning.

By then Wilma was sixteen years old, the youngest girl at the camp. She still had some growing to do and couldn't match the endurance or strength of the older, more experienced runners. When she ran, she clenched her fists and pumped her arms like a windmill. Coach Temple rode her constantly, yelling at her to stretch her legs, stop clenching her fists, and keep her arms close to her body. "Stretch out those long legs," he would shout, "stride!"

For two long and hard weeks, the cross-country training continued. The coach was merciless, pushing Wilma to the breaking point emotionally and physically. But when she was feeling lowest, he picked her up with encouraging words, telling her she had the potential to be a champion. Wilma had many thoughts of giving up, but her mother's determination to care for her as a sick child always came to mind. If she quit, her mother's many years of care and treatment would seem wasted. She could never return home to disappoint her mother.

Eventually, the cross-country running put Wilma in top condition. She began breathing easily and naturally during runs.

After two weeks of endurance runs, the team started in on 50-, 100-, and 200-meter sprints, with runners racing side by side down the oval track. Wilma learned the most important thing about sprints: the start. The coach taught her to relax, get loose, and calm down her body before a race. She took deep, steady breaths; shook her arms, legs, and torso; and moved her head from side to side.

> TSU's big track star before Wilma Rudolph was Mae Faggs, the first woman to compete in three different Olympic Games: 1948, 1952, and 1956.

But the start itself was her weak point. For the first time in her track career, she used devices called starting blocks. The blocks supported her feet at an angle, allowing her to push off at the sound of the starting gun. But it took Wilma a long time to get used to the blocks, and her reflexes weren't precise. She had trouble getting off the starting line clean and fast. Her long legs unbent in an awkward manner, which prevented her from getting any speed up until several strides into the race.

Because of her awkward starts, Wilma did poorly in the short sprints, such as the 50-meter race. She did much better in the longer sprints, when she had a few seconds more to correct a bad start. She had a lot of strength at the end of her races, when her legs delivered a powerful kick that drove her past the other runners.

She was still not in condition to beat older runners in sprint races. But Coach Temple saw a lot of potential in Wilma. He wasn't much for praise or even talking. But when he said nothing after a race or a workout, Wilma knew that meant he was satisfied with her performance.

Coach Temple saw Wilma as a good relay runner. He placed her on a junior relay team with three other high school girls. The team ran a 400-meter race, with each member running 100 meters and passing on a metal baton to the next runner.

Relay races are some of the most exciting events in track. Speed and skill are involved, and the baton handoff gives a few moments of suspense as the runners struggle to coordinate their movements. Relays are crowd favorites. For that reason, track meets always schedule relays at the end of the competition.

Wilma learned that running a relay was a lot more complicated than running a solo sprint. The handoff, not the start, was the key. Everyone handled the baton a little differently. Everyone had a different style, and the team members had to know one another's style. The runner passing the baton had to hold the baton steady so that the next runner could easily grab it and go. Team members practiced the handoff hundreds of times, first walking through it, then jogging easily, then running harder, and then sprinting flat out. Wilma's high school team was good enough to give the TSU college relay team a very tough race, even tougher as the summer went on.

For most of the summer, the Tigerbelles and the high schoolers competed only against one another. These races were supposed to prepare the runners for keener competition to come. Coach Temple had each side wear a blue or a white uniform. He kept score and made sure everyone on campus knew about the meets. The stands filled up with summer-session students eager to see some good running.

RELAY HISTORY

According to historians, relay races began in ancient Greece. During some religious ceremonies, torchbearers passed their torches from one runner to the next—always careful never to drop the torches. The torch relay became a part of ancient athletic contests, although never part of the ancient Olympic Games.

The first modern relay meet, the Penn Relays, began in 1895. In 1924 the Olympics held its first relay race. Modern relays always have four athletes on a side.

The coach knew that the crowd in the stands was an important part of training. Wilma and the other young runners learned to deal with the attention of spectators. They learned how to concentrate and block out the noise of strangers who were yelling and cheering for them or their opponents to win the race.

Thousands of spectators would be looking on at the end of the summer, when Coach Temple took his young runners to a national AAU (Amateur Athletic Union) meet in Philadelphia, Pennsylvania. The coach worked the team harder than ever as the competition drew near. He moved Wilma to the anchor leg of her relay team. This was the final leg, which had to be run by the fastest runner on the team. By the end of the summer, she had mastered the handoff and the final sprint to the finish line.

Finally, the time came. The Tigerbelles and the high schoolers climbed into a caravan of station wagons. They hit the road for Philadelphia, with Wilma sitting next to Coach Temple, giving directions from a road map.

It was Wilma's first trip out of the South. In Philadelphia, the big city awed her and made her feel small. Huge buildings of iron and concrete towered into the sky. The city streets were noisy and crowded with traffic and people. The sprawling neighborhoods of brick row houses seemed to go on for miles.

The stadium at Franklin Field, where the track meet took place, was filled with thousands of fans, all with their eyes on the track and the runners. Wilma had never experienced anything like it.

QUALIFYING HEATS

In track competition, several dozen runners may be competing for a single first-place prize. But tracks have only eight or nine lanes, so all the runners can't race at the same time. To narrow down the field, track meets include a series of races called qualifying heats. Runners who come in first, second, or third in the first heat pass on to the next heat, the semifinals. The runners with the best times in the semifinal heats advance to the finals. (Depending on the size of the field, some events have additional qualifying heats.)

Wilma and the other high schoolers had their races on the first day of the meet. Wilma ran in the 75- and 100-meter sprints and the 4x100-meter relay. She may have been nervous and a little intimidated by the surroundings, but she ran as well as she ever had. She won the two qualifying heats (preliminary races) in the two sprint distances, then won the final races as well. She and the other high schoolers also won their relay event. Wilma didn't lose a single heat all day long.

The wins at Philadelphia let Wilma forget about her last big meet, in Tuskegee, Alabama. The humiliation of losing that day was gone, replaced by a much better feeling: winning. A summer of training and work had paid off big, and she even heard some words of encouragement from quiet Coach Temple.

The real highlight came on the second day of the meet. A race official came over to talk to Coach Temple and ask him a favor. He had a couple of professional baseball players on the field that day, and he wanted to have their picture taken with some runners from the TSU team. The coach agreed and picked Wilma for the picture.

Feeling shy and not really wanting to talk, Wilma walked over to greet Don Newcombe and Jackie Robinson, two of the star players from the Brooklyn Dodgers baseball team. Robinson was the first African American to play major league baseball in the twentieth century. He was a hero to African Americans everywhere—and here he was right next to a shy high school girl from Clarksville.

Jackie Robinson spoke first. He had been watching the meet, even the junior races, and he praised Wilma for her running style. He thought she had the potential to be a great runner. In fact, in his opinion, she was one of the best college runners he had seen. Then she surprised him with some news: she was still only a high schooler!

Robinson had a simple message for Wilma Rudolph that day. Whatever you do, he told her, just keep running. Don't let anything hold you back. All the way back to Clarksville, Wilma thought about this short moment, meeting and talking to Jackie Robinson, having her picture taken with him. He was a black man who had broken a very old barrier: the ban on African Americans in big-league baseball. He had done it with talent, work, and a lot of courage. He showed her, and every other young black athlete, that it could be done, that times were changing, and that anything was possible. Wilma would never forget that day or that lesson.

Chapter Five

Young Olympian

Wilma's next meet that summer took place in Ponca City, Oklahoma. Again, Wilma competed with the summer camp high school team. She and her teammates rode a bus with the college runners all the way from Nashville to Oklahoma. At the meet, Wilma took part in the relay, again helping her team to a win. The rest of the TSU team did just as well, winning every single sprint and relay at the meet.

In just a few years, Coach Temple had made TSU into the best women's track team in the country. But the victory at Ponca City didn't win the team respect away from the stadium and the running track. It was still a time of segregation, for winners as well as losers. On the way back to Nashville, the team stopped at a restaurant in Kansas for lunch. At first, the restaurant turned them away. The restaurant served only white people—not African Americans.

For many of the young women, this was just business as usual. On the road, they often had to buy lunch at a store and eat it on the bus or sit at a picnic area reserved for African Americans. Again, Wilma felt the humiliation of being treated differently just because of the color of her skin.

But this time things were different. Angry, the white bus driver climbed down from his seat and had words with the restaurant owners. He explained that his passengers had just won a national track championship. Surely, the restaurant could open its doors for them. The bus driver won his argument, and the Tigerbelles had their lunch, sitting down in the restaurant like everyone else.

During her summer of training with Ed Temple, Wilma and the other athletes ran one hundred miles a week.

After Wilma's wins in Philadelphia and Ponca City, Coach Temple believed she was ready to try out for the U.S. Olympic squad. She was still only sixteen. But he felt she had the experience and ability to compete against the best in the world. Her junior year at Burt High wouldn't start for a few weeks. She had the time for the tryouts, and she was in great shape after training all summer long at Tennessee State.

THE ANCIENT AND MODERN OLYMPICS

The Olympic Games are a giant meeting of the best amateur athletes from all over the world. The Games date to ancient Greece, when cities sent their best runners, wrestlers, chariot drivers, and other athletes to compete at the town of Olympia. After the Roman Empire conquered Greece, the Roman emperor banned the ancient Olympics.

In 1896 a Frenchman named Pierre de Coubertin revived the Olympic Games. The modern Games are designed to be a time of pure amateur sports, when the world's best athletes meet in a spirit of friendly competition, free of politics and other rivalries.

Wilma knew very little about the Olympic Games. For someone from Clarksville, Tennessee, the Olympics were a distant event. They took place only once every four years—the last time in 1952, in Helsinki, Finland. She had seen a few articles in the local newspaper and had heard some news of the Olympics on the radio. But as a kid growing up and then as a high school basketball player, Wilma never took much notice of the Games.

That year the Olympic Trials took place in Seattle, Washington. Late in the summer of 1956, Coach Temple, Wilma, and a group of college runners piled into a station wagon for a long drive. This time they were going all the way to the West Coast and cloudy, cool Seattle.

Wilma was the kid of the squad. She looked up to all the college students—especially Mae Faggs. Mae was the strongest runner on the Tigerbelles. She had already been to the Olympics twice, winning a gold medal in the 4x100-meter relay in 1952. Wilma and Mae became good friends. When they raced against each other in practice, Wilma often slowed down out of politeness, finishing a close second to her friend.

For Mae, the Olympic trials in Seattle were business as usual. But Wilma had never seen so many officials and judges and never before had had the attention of the press and reporters. She felt nervous, which made her muscles tense and her breathing shallow. Mae offered Wilma a lot of advice about dealing with the pressure. With Mae's help, Wilma tried to put the pressure and the cold weather out of her mind.

Coach Temple entered Wilma in the 200-meter dash and the 4x100-meter relays. One of her opponents in the 200 would be her friend Mae Faggs. At the starting line, Wilma stood right next to her Tigerbelle teammate. "Stick with me," Mae told her. "You stick with me in the race, you make the team." The two ran step for step all the way to the tape, winding up in a dead-even tie for first place.

In this race, Wilma showed that she could run with Mae Faggs or anyone else. With her first-place tie, she had made the Olympic team. After the race, Mae gave her some news: after the upcoming Olympics, she was going to retire. She had run enough and done enough, and she was ready to stop. In Wilma Rudolph, she had finally found a runner who could replace her—maybe even *beat* her—at the biggest track meet of all, the Summer Olympic Games.

Mae Faggs was nicknamed Little Mae. She was five feet, two inches tall.

When Wilma returned to Clarksville, she found herself suddenly famous. Strangers knew who she was, and many of them came up to wish her good luck in the Games. Burt High School gave her permission to travel, train, and compete instead of attending school. Some people contacted Coach Gray, offering to help Wilma buy good clothes and luggage for the trip. Her parents didn't have much money, and Wilma accepted the help gratefully.

In October 1956, Wilma flew to Los Angeles, California, to gather with the rest of the Olympic track team. At age sixteen, she was the youngest member of the team. They would spend two weeks training and preparing at the University of Southern California (USC).

The women's Olympic track coach, Nel Jackson, was from the Tuskegee Institute. But Coach Temple was in Los Angeles too. He offered advice to the Tennessee State runners and helped Jackson train the team.

Coach Jackson was all business. She put Wilma on the 4x100-meter relay team with Mae Faggs, Isabelle Daniels, and Margaret Mathews. Wilma would run in the third position, and Margaret would run the anchor leg. Wilma would also run on her own in the 200-meter race.

Workouts took place in the morning. In the afternoon, Wilma was free to walk around the USC campus or go back to her hotel and relax. During her time off, she read newspaper and magazine articles about the upcoming Games, learning as much as she could about the Olympics and its traditions.

The 1956 Summer Olympic Games were scheduled for Melbourne, Australia. Since Australia is in the Southern Hemisphere (where the seasons are the opposite of those in the Northern Hemisphere), the Games took place in November and December—springtime in Australia. Australia had prepared new

46

tracks and stadiums for the events and built housing for the teams arriving from all over the world.

Although Melbourne hosted the Olympics in 1956, a few events were held in Europe. To prevent disease, Australia had strict regulations about bringing foreign horses into the country. For this reason, the equestrian, or horseback, events took place in Sweden.

The trip to Australia was a long and tiring journey. After the U.S. team broke camp in Los Angeles, they flew to Hawaii, then to the Fiji Islands in the middle of the Pacific Ocean. (At the time, Australia was impossible to reach in a single flight.) In Fiji Wilma saw a whole nation of black people, all speaking a foreign language that she couldn't understand. The trip made Wilma realize that the world was a very big place—and there was much more to it than what she knew in Clarksville, Tennessee.

Finally Wilma and the U.S. Olympic team arrived in Melbourne. Wilma felt excited and very curious about this distant country. The first thing she noticed was that people spoke English with the peculiar accent of Australia. It sounded somewhat British, but it also reminded her of the southern drawl of her hometown.

And Wilma noticed something even better: integration, the mixing of different races in public places. Olympic officials offered mixed tables and sleeping quarters for black and white athletes. Blacks and whites mingled together in the Olympic Village and other places. Wilma had grown up with segregation and with the feeling that whites would always be against her. Australia made her realize that the world didn't have to be like that.

In the Olympic Village, she roomed with her teammates on the women's track team. They had to be in their rooms at nine o'clock every night. There were strict rules against late-night parties, but that didn't stop Wilma from meeting athletes from Asia, Latin America, Africa, and Europe.

The Olympics that year included more than three thousand athletes from sixty-seven countries, all young adults and teenagers, all in good condition, all the best in their countries at their events. Wilma had never seen so many different people or heard so many foreign languages. She saw dark and light skin, hair of many colors, different clothes on nearly everyone she met. But everyone had the same goal: to win an Olympic medal.

"I began to realize that the world was bigger than Clarksville," Wilma later wrote. "I said to myself, 'You're lucky, you're luckier than all of the kids back home, because you're getting to see all of these things and they're not.'"

For one week, Wilma trained at starts, at relays, and at getting used to the weather and the surroundings. The team had no set schedule for practices. Team members simply worked out as long as they could, every day. Everyone was eager and helpful. One day the official starter (the person who signals the start of a track race), an Australian, arrived to practice with the U.S. track team. He ran through a start, making sure that everyone got used to his voice and his Australian accent.

THE GOLDEN GIRL

Australian Betty Cuthbert, known as the Golden Girl for her blond hair, became a hero in Australia for her three wins at the 1956 Melbourne Olympics. She was only eighteen years old at the time. Four years later, she prepared to return to the Olympics in Rome, but an injury prevented her from competing. In 1964 Cuthbert returned to the Olympic Games, this time in Tokyo, Japan. She was twenty-six years old, and many people thought she was too old to win anything. But she ran a brilliant 400-meter race and brought home another gold medal.

After the opening-day parade, Wilma also met Betty Cuthbert, an Australian track star. Everyone expected Cuthbert to win all the women's running events that year. Cuthbert was confident and very, very fast. She also had a secret weapon: kangaroo leather. Her beautiful white track shoes were made from the tanned skin of kangaroos, animals native to Australia. They were soft and light to the touch. Wilma felt envious when she saw them and realized that her own cow-leather shoes were not nearly as light and comfortable.

THE NOT-SO-FRIENDLY GAMES

The Olympic Games are supposed to be about friendly athletic competition between nations. But often, politics interfere. For instance, in 1956 teams from the Soviet Union and Hungary competed with each other, but not in a friendly manner. The Soviet army had just invaded Hungary to put down a rebellion. The Hungarians were angry with the Soviets.

During an Olympic water polo match, Soviet and Hungarian athletes fought bitterly in the water. Even the crowd became unruly. The match was called off in the last minute after one player punched another in the eye. At that point, Hungary led 4–0. Hungary eventually won the gold, but not before a lot of blood was spilled in Melbourne's water polo pool.

Cuthbert played fair, telling Wilma about the shop where she could buy a pair. But the shoes cost thirty dollars, an amount Wilma couldn't afford. Although her teammate Mae Faggs offered to buy her a pair, Wilma didn't want to accept the money. She would run the best she could, in her own American shoes.

The practices weren't always a success. The Tigerbelles missed Coach Temple, who hadn't accompanied them to Australia. The relay runners struggled with their handoffs. Passing the baton while running at top speed is always tricky, but for some reason, the team had more trouble than usual. Their handoffs were clumsy. More than once, a runner dropped the baton on the ground—a sure way to lose precious seconds. The women worked hard, motivating one another with words of encouragement. They got angry when a teammate didn't seem to be doing her best.

On the third day of the Olympics, Wilma ran her first race, a qualifying heat for the 200-meter sprint. The top three runners would advance to the semifinals. Wilma ran a good race and finished third. In the semis, only the first two finishers would continue to the finals. The pressure was on, and the eyes of Wilma's teammates and the stadium crowd were on her. She felt nervous, a feeling that shortened her breath and tightened her muscles. She couldn't relax and get the easy, flowing motion that allowed her to win races. She finished third in the semifinals, dropping out of the competition.

The loss in the 200-meter semifinal left her feeling depressed and frustrated. She stayed in her room, not eating or sleeping and feeling like a complete failure. But the race was over, and there was nothing she could do about it. She could only look forward to the relay race.

In the meantime, Wilma sat in the stands as a spectator, watching Betty Cuthbert run like the wind. Cuthbert was at the top of her form, winning gold medals in the 100- and 200-meter races. Wilma watched her closely, envying her success and her medals and vowing that she would be at the next Olympics, no matter where it was. She would train for four straight years, she would run faster than anybody, and she would win.

Without Coach Temple with her in Melbourne, watching her and guiding her, Wilma felt a little adrift. The loss in the 200-meter heat made the feeling worse. But Betty Cuthbert's performance inspired her and brought back her enthusiasm. She felt eager to compete once again. On the day of the relay, she and her teammates psyched themselves up with positive words. As the minutes and hours passed, Wilma got her confidence back.

Six teams were spread around the track. Wilma would be in the third position for the United States. The gun for the 4x100-meter relay went off. Mae Faggs ran the first leg, passing the baton off to Margaret Mathews, who ran to pass it off to Wilma. But they had trouble with the handoff. She and Margaret bobbled the baton, and Wilma had to slow down to get a grip on it. The mistake caused a crucial loss of speed. When she turned forward again, Wilma ran flat out, her legs driving in their long, powerful strides. She handed the baton to the anchor runner, Isabelle Daniels, who sped off toward the tape.

THE FRIENDLY GAMES

On the last day of the Melbourne Olympics, Wilma marched in the closing ceremonies. For the first time in Olympic history, athletes from different countries mingled together in the closing parade and didn't march as separate teams. The mingling helped give the 1956 Olympics the nickname the Friendly Games. It was the idea of an Australian teenager, John Wing, who had suggested it in a letter to the Melbourne Olympic Committee. Olympic athletes still follow this friendly custom.

But the Australian team was just too good. Betty Cuthbert crossed the finish line with a new world-record time of 44.5 seconds, just a half step ahead of Britain's Heather Armitage. The U.S. team finished in third place, right behind the British team. They had won a bronze medal.

Wilma climbed onto the medal stand with her teammates. She bowed her head as an Olympic official placed the bronze medal around her neck. The women stood at attention as the Australian national anthem played over loudspeakers, in honor of the gold-medal-winning Australian team.

The medal ceremony was a moment Wilma would never forget. But the ceremony also gave her a pang of regret. She knew she could do much, much better.

The end of the Games saddened Wilma and her teammates. They had to leave behind new friends. The excitement of the Olympics became just a memory. But Wilma couldn't let go of the feeling that she had unfinished business at the Olympic Games. She was just a high school kid from a little town in Tennessee, but she had an Olympic medal, and she had four years to get ready to earn another one—made of gold.

Chapter | Six

Back to Tennessee

After the long return flight to the United States, Wilma arrived home to Tennessee. In the eyes of her parents and friends, she was a star. Burt High School closed down for a day and held a special assembly just to honor her. "They [her classmates] passed my bronze medal around," she told a reporter, "so that everyone could touch, feel, and see what an Olympic medal is like. When I got it back, there were handprints all over it."

When classes and practices started up again, everyone treated her a little differently. They looked at her with respect and, often, jealousy. Wilma felt the eyes on her and felt the pressure of living up to her reputation. Some friends dropped away, while others wanted to show off by saying they knew her. Stardom was an uncomfortable, unfamiliar feeling. Wilma just wanted to be treated like the same old Skeeter she'd always been.

By this time, Wilma was in the top shape of her life. With her friend Nancy Bowen, she led the Burt High School basketball team through one of the greatest seasons in Tennessee basketball history. The team won every single game it played. Wilma averaged 35 points a game, shooting an incredible 49 points in her season-high game. At the state tournament in Nashville, Burt sailed past its opponents as Coach Gray shouted from the sidelines and Wilma dropped one shot after another through the net.

The six-on-six format for girls high school basketball remained the rule in Tennessee until 1980, when the state switched to a five-on-five game.

After the basketball season, track started up in the spring of 1957. This time sixteen-year-old Wilma felt more pressure than before to perform at every practice and every race. She was an Olympic medalist, and she was expected to beat everybody, all the time. The medal intimidated her opponents, who thought they had no chance against her. They simply dropped out of their races or ran without really trying to win. Wilma won every meet she entered that year. Winning became routine and almost boring. To motivate herself, she remembered the vow she had made in Melbourne—to prepare for the next Olympics.

Wilma looked forward to the prom that year. At Burt High School, both juniors and seniors attended. Robert Eldridge asked her to go with him to the dance. Because she didn't have enough money to buy a new dress, she borrowed one from Shirley Crowder, a friend from Tennessee State. The long blue dress looked beautiful with a white orchid that Robert gave her to wear.

The dance took place in the high school gym. For many students, it was the first chance in their lives to dress up, dance with their friends, and get away from the rules and watchful eyes of their parents. After the dance, Robert, Wilma, and some friends escaped Clarksville. They drove their cars to a nightclub in Kentucky, about twenty-five miles away. At about one in the morning, after a couple of hours spent dancing at the club, they headed back home, speeding all the way.

It was a very dangerous moment. Robert and Wilma made it home safely, but Wilma's friend and basketball teammate, Nancy Bowen, did not. The driver of the car she was riding in lost control at high speed and smashed head-on into a bridge support. Nancy and the driver were killed instantly.

That night, Coach Gray called Wilma with the news. Nancy's death left Wilma shocked and stunned. She felt sad and empty for a long time. She returned to Coach Temple's camp at Tennessee State that summer, but she had a hard time keeping her focus on track.

The coach could see that Wilma had her mind on other things. He went easy and left her alone. He let her know that he understood her sadness. That summer was one of the toughest times of Wilma's life. She later wrote that Nancy's death was "my first experience with tragedy. I couldn't handle it. I was an emotional wreck."

When Wilma returned to Burt High for her senior year, she got back into the routine of classes and practices. She began to feel better. The thought of competing again got her mind off the loss of her friend and steeled her for the tough training she knew lay ahead.

By then, as Coach Temple had predicted, Wilma had won a scholarship to Tennessee State University. The school would pay her tuition as long as she graduated from high school, kept her grades up at TSU, and ran for the Tigerbelles. She would also have to work at a part-time job on campus. With the encouragement of her parents, Wilma filled out the paperwork necessary for attendance at Tennessee State. She knew that education was the key to a better future, a life away from the poverty she had known as a child. She prepared herself for the busy life of a college student.

Six-year-old Wilma Rudolph *(right)* poses with her sister Yvonne.

As a member of the basketball team and the track team, Wilma was a star athlete at Burt High School.

Wilma was just sixteen years old when she took part in the 1956 Olympic Games in Melbourne, Australia. It was also her first brush with fame. Sometimes she and her teammates stood for hours signing autographs.

Wilma pushes off the starting blocks in the opening heat of the 200-meter race at the 1960 Olympics in Rome, Italy. She set a new Olympic record of 23.2 seconds in this heat.

© POPPERFOTO/Alamy

© Central Press/Getty Images

In the 200-meter final, Wilma *(far right)* finished in 24.0 seconds to win her second gold medal of the 1960 Olympic Games.

The gold-medal-winning 400-meter relay team stands together on the Olympic podium. They are *(left to right):* Wilma Rudolph, Barbara Jones, Lucinda Williams, and Martha Hudson.

Wilma Rudolph returned home from the 1960 Olympics to be greeted with several parades, including this one in Nashville, Tennessee.

Wilma's oldest daughter, Yolanda *(left),* earned a scholarship to Tennessee State University and ran briefly as a Tigerbelle. She's pictured with Wilma *(right).*

This statue, showing Wilma's stride as she crosses the finish line in a race, stands in Wilma's hometown of Clarksville, Tennessee.

Her senior year promised to be one of the most carefree of Wilma's life. She had survived polio and a tough childhood. She played basketball as well as any young woman in Tennessee. She was in great physical shape, one of the fastest runners in the country, and a medal-winning veteran of the Olympic Games. Everything was going well for her. With her scholarship assured, she just had to keep her grades up, graduate, and get ready for college.

ED TEMPLE'S WINNING CAREER

Ed Temple coached the Tennessee State Tigerbelles for forty-three years, until his retirement in 1993. He coached forty Olympic runners, who won a total of twenty-three medals, including thirteen golds. Coach Temple was proud of the fact that of the forty Olympians he coached, all but one made it through to graduation. The Tigerbelles remain dominant in women's track to this day.

Then the very unexpected happened. Wilma sat quietly in the office of her family doctor, Dr. Coleman. He told her the news: she was pregnant. She was due to have a baby in the summer of 1958. The baby's father was her boyfriend, Robert Eldridge.

The doctor promised not to tell anybody. He would leave it up to Wilma to handle the situation as best she could. She wanted to have the baby, but she couldn't bring herself to tell her mother, her father, or anybody else. Her father, she knew, would be furious with her. He might force her to quit school. He might even throw her out of the house.

The weeks and months went by. As the pregnancy advanced, she began to feel sick. At basketball practices, Coach Gray noticed that she was slowing down. Then Wilma began to gain weight, which hurt her speed and reflexes. The coach talked to Dr. Coleman. The doctor mentioned that Wilma had a "stomach tumor." The coach knew right away what he really meant.

Coach Gray took Wilma aside and gave her some advice. Having a baby was more important than basketball, he told her. Wilma would have to forget about sports for a while. She would have to tell her family immediately. Wilma gathered her courage and told her older sister Yvonne about the pregnancy. Finally she told her mother and father.

Wilma's parents reacted calmly, but her father banned Robert from her life. Wilma dropped out of basketball and track. She didn't run a stride that spring or summer. She graduated from Burt High in May 1958. In July she had a baby girl, whom she named Yolanda. She brought Yolanda home from the hospital and began to prepare for her first year at Tennessee State.

Wilma knew that Coach Temple had a rule: no mothers on his track team. But for Wilma, he waived the rule. Grateful and eager to compete again, Wilma made arrangements for her sister Yvonne to take care of her daughter. Yvonne, who lived in Saint Louis, Missouri, had a son in nursery school. She was a full-time homemaker, so she had the time to take care of her sister's baby girl.

Robert, Yolanda's father, wanted to marry Wilma and make her a housewife. But Wilma resisted. She didn't want to give up her dream of returning to the Olympics—and this time winning a race and a gold medal. And her father wouldn't hear of marriage of any kind. He didn't want Wilma seeing Robert ever again. It was a difficult time for Wilma and Robert.

❝*I discovered that bronze doesn't shine. So, I decided, I'm going to try this one more time. I'm going to go for the gold.*❞

—WILMA RUDOLPH

The baby was safe with Yvonne. In fact, after a few months, Yvonne declared that she wanted to adopt Yolanda as her own child. At the thought of losing her baby, Wilma felt deep anguish and a mother's protective anger. Against her father's

61

wishes, Wilma and Robert drove to Saint Louis and took Yolanda back. Wilma's mother agreed to take care of Yolanda while Wilma attended college in Nashville. Yolanda seemed to charm everyone around her. After a short while, even Wilma's father fell in love with her.

Chapter | Seven

Gold-Medal Girl

To keep her scholarship at Tennessee State, Wilma had to maintain a 2.0 grade-point average. She also had to work two hours a day, five days a week, at various jobs around campus. Her days were full, from dawn to evening, with classes, study, work, and practice sessions. When the track team had a meet in another town, she had to keep studying, even as she rode the bus, stayed in hotels, and trained.

By her sophomore year, which began in the fall of 1959, nineteen-year-old Wilma was spending all her spare time on the school's outdoor track. At five foot eleven and about 130 pounds, she was the tallest, strongest, and fastest member of the Tigerbelles. A strange thing had happened since she had given birth: she was running faster than she ever had!

Like any athlete, she had to worry about injuries. At a meet between U.S. and Soviet athletes in 1959, Wilma pulled a thigh muscle, which put her out of the competition. In early 1960, she had to have her tonsils taken out, and she suffered a violent reaction to the surgery. But Wilma remained determined to make the Olympic team. She never forgot the vow she had made to herself in Melbourne.

The first big meet of 1960 was an AAU meet in Corpus Christi, Texas. If she did well at this meet, Wilma would be invited to the Olympic Trials at Texas Christian University. By this time, Wilma had recovered from her tonsil surgery and had few worries about her running. She was strong, in shape, and very fast. Behind her were several years of hard training, Olympic experience, and the expert coaching of Ed Temple. Ahead of her were the Olympic Games, which would be held in Rome, Italy, later that year.

In Corpus Christi, Wilma ran a good race in the 200 meters. She broke the tape ahead of everyone else and went to sit by quiet Coach Temple. She took a look up at her time, which was posted on the side of the track, but paid no special attention to it. Meanwhile, the coach congratulated her for the win and said nothing else. A few minutes later, one of Wilma's teammates came over to her. Why wasn't she celebrating? She had just run the 200 meters in 22.9 seconds—a new world record! Wilma hadn't known what the record was when the race began. She had set the record without even knowing it.

Wilma's world-record time of 22.9 seconds in the 200-meter race, set in Corpus Christi, Texas, stood for five years. In 1965 Irena Kriszenstein set a new mark of 22.7 seconds in Warsaw, Poland.

At the Olympic Trials that summer, Wilma qualified for the Olympic team in the 100-meter, 200-meter, and relay events. The relay team was made up of four women from Tennessee State, with Wilma as the anchor runner. And the Olympic coach would be TSU's Ed Temple. The Tigerbelle women's track team had finally come into its own. Every female U.S. Olympic runner that year was from TSU.

To prepare for the games, the Olympic track team trained at Kansas State University. In the first week, Temple ran his team through three workouts a day. He then cut their workouts down to two a day, then one a day. He wanted Wilma and her teammates in the best shape of their lives, but he didn't want to push them too hard.

When the 1960 Olympic Games opened in Rome, the U.S. team boasted some of the world's best athletes. Their confidence was high, and rivalries were keen, especially between the U.S. and Soviet athletes. At the time, the United States and the

Soviet Union were competing fiercely to see which one was the strongest country in the world.

Wilma again found herself in a strange foreign city. But Rome was different from Melbourne in many ways. Scattered around the city were ancient Roman ruins, including the Colosseum, a huge stadium. Wilma also saw beautiful old churches filled with paintings and sculpture. She saw the Vatican, home of the pope, the head of the Catholic Church. The traffic in the city was crazy and noisy, but the people were friendly. They spoke a foreign language, Italian, and used it to greet the Olympic athletes they recognized.

The Rome Olympics were the first to be broadcast on U.S. television, by the CBS network. The network taped the most important events in Rome, then rushed the tapes by plane to its New York City studios every evening for broadcast to the nation.

At the Olympic Village, Wilma again met athletes from all over the world. She mingled with them during practices and in the evening, when they attended dances, parties, and dinners. At one meeting of the entire U.S. team, with athletes from every sport, Wilma met a young boxer named Cassius Clay. He hailed from Louisville, Kentucky. Clay was boastful. He told everyone he was going to win a gold medal. But when he was around Wilma, Clay acted nervous and shy. (Clay would later change his name to Muhammad Ali.)

Coach Temple ran tough practices every day to get the women's team ready. The weather was hot, with temperatures sometimes running over 100 degrees. The weather didn't bother Wilma, because she was used to the summer heat in Tennessee. In fact, the heat and the intense sun reminded her of home and relaxed her. She was at the top of her form. She had the potential to win three gold medals, a feat that no U.S. runner had ever accomplished in the Olympic Games.

Wilma's best competition at Melbourne, Betty Cuthbert, had suffered an injury and had withdrawn from the Games. Wilma really had to worry about just one competitor: Jutta Heine, a West German track star who was just as tall and just as fast as Wilma or anyone else on Coach Temple's squad.

Nothing else stood in Wilma's way, except maybe her own high spirits. On the day before she was to run her first race, the 100-meter sprint, she joined her teammates in a little fun, running through water sprinklers on a grassy stretch of ground near the Olympic Stadium. The day was hot, and leaping through the water cooled them off. But then Wilma took a bad jump, landing in a small hole in the ground that she hadn't seen.

The fall bruised her ankle. The pain was bad—but even worse was the fear that she had spoiled the best chance of her entire career. The team doctor immediately packed Wilma's ankle in ice to reduce the swelling. Her teammates carried her back to her room. She kept off the foot for the rest of the day and through the night. The next morning, she rose from bed very carefully and gingerly put some weight on the foot.

She felt the slight sprain. It might hurt in a turn, but it wouldn't keep her from running on a straightaway. That day, she was scheduled for the qualifying heats in the 100 meters, a short sprint with no turns. She boarded the bus to the Olympic Stadium, with Coach Temple by her side, giving her calm words of reassurance. When the bus finally arrived at the stadium, she climbed carefully down the bus steps with her teammates.

With runners from several other teams, Wilma made her way through a long, dark tunnel to the field. At the end of the tunnel, she came out into an enormous stadium, filled with eighty thousand spectators. In the days leading up to her first event, the Italian press had been running stories about her, along with her photograph. The fans knew who she was, and they were looking for her.

A chant went up. "Vil-ma, Vil-ma," the crowd shouted. Before she had run a single race, thousands of people were shouting her name.

Wilma put the crowd and the chanting out of her mind. When a race official called her name, she walked to the starting line, thinking only about running and winning. Despite the sore ankle, she easily beat her competition in both qualifying heats that day.

On the following day, she advanced to the final qualifying heat. By this time, her ankle wasn't bothering her at all. She won the race in a time of 11 seconds flat—faster than the world record. But a slight breeze had been blowing at her back, making her run faster. In sprints, a tailwind of more than 2.0 meters per second cancels out a chance for a world record. So Wilma's time got her to the finals, but it didn't count as a record.

❝ *They called me the 'Black Gazelle' in Rome, and I thought that was wonderful. I didn't find it offensive at all, because I knew they weren't just speaking of color. They were speaking of something beautiful in color and motion.*❞

—WILMA RUDOLPH

On Saturday, September 7, Wilma walked through the tunnel at the Olympic Stadium for the 100-meter finals. She and five other women stood at the starting line as the crowd looked on and cheered. Wilma's best competitors were Jutta Heine, from West Germany, and the British runner Dorothy Hyman. The crowd grew silent as the starter raised his gun. Wilma recalled the practice sessions with the starter calling out "on your mark" and "ready" in Italian. She pushed her feet hard against the starting blocks and waited.

The starting gun fired. Wilma's start was good. Her legs unwound from the crouch and hit their long, easy strides. At 50 meters, she was reaching the front of the pack. Her powerful finishing kick began. She felt no pain at all from her bruised ankle. She was 5 meters ahead of Dorothy Hyman at the finish line. It was an easy win—once again in the record time of 11 seconds flat—and her first gold medal.

The moment the race was over, telegrams of congratulations began arriving at the Olympic Village. One telegram came from Betty Cuthbert, who had watched the race on television from her home in Australia. Photographers and reporters arrived at Wilma's room, begging for pictures and interviews. Flowers from well-wishers were laid out on the tables and chairs. The rest of the day, crowds of admirers followed her everywhere. In exactly 11 seconds, Wilma had become an international celebrity.

Coach Temple brought her back to earth. She had more races to run. The 200-meter final was scheduled for Tuesday,

September 10. She had only a few days to rest up and take care of her ankle.

When September 10 finally arrived, the weather turned bad. The sky was gray and rainy. The air was cool. Wilma took longer than usual to warm up. But when she got to the starting line, she was ready and confident. She had already won the 100-meter sprint, meaning she was officially the fastest woman in the world. If she ran the race she was capable of running, nobody could beat her in the 200.

Nobody did. Wilma ran flat out—around the turn and down the straight to the finish—for 200 meters. None of the other runners, including Dorothy Hyman and Jutta Heine, even came close. Her time was 24 seconds exactly—not quite the world-record 22.9 she had been running in the trials, but good enough. At the awards ceremony, she stood to attention while the U.S. national anthem played and her second gold medal dangled around her neck.

Wilma had one more race to run: the 4x100-meter relay. In that race, despite a bad handoff between Wilma and third-leg runner Lucinda Williams, Wilma carried her team to the finish line for another gold medal.

Wilma Rudolph had become the first American woman to win three gold medals at the Olympic Games. Her feat made her the star of the Rome Olympics. Photographers mobbed her at the victory stand, and the crowd shouted her name. She had a hard time pulling away and finding her way back to the bus and the Olympic Village. It seemed that all eyes were on her, and everyone wanted her time and attention.

HER BEST SHOT

Right after Wilma's triumph in the 4x100 relay, shot-putter Earlene Brown, a stocky woman from Texas, gave her hearty congratulations. Earlene shook Wilma's hand. "Honey, I knew you'd do it. Now old Earlene better get a move on herself," Brown said, referring to her own upcoming shot put event. She went out to throw the shot farther than she ever had, nearly 47 feet. The throw was good enough for a bronze medal, making Earlene Brown the only American woman ever to win an Olympic medal in the shot put.

Her fame was just beginning. European newspaper reporters adored her and gave her nicknames, such as La Gazella Nera ("the Black Gazelle" in Italian), La Perle Noire ("the Black Pearl" in French), and the Chattanooga Choo Choo (a reference to a famous Tennessee train). They described her training, her practice runs, her every waking moment. People in the streets of Rome asked for her autograph and picture. Coaches from the other U.S. Olympic squads wanted to shake her hand, as did her rivals from the other women's track teams. With the rest of the U.S. Olympic team, she was invited to the Vatican to meet Pope John XXIII.

Wilma was overwhelmed—and ready to go home. But as much as she wanted to leave, she had to stay in Europe. Coach Temple had arranged for Wilma and the team to run in the British Empire Games in London, England. England was cold, gray, and damp. It couldn't match the excitement or the warmth—in the air or in the attitude of the people—of Rome.

In addition to her gold medals, Wilma Rudolph earned many honors in 1960. The Associated Press named her its Woman Athlete of the Year. The Italian government gave her the Christopher Columbus Award for Most Outstanding International Sports Personality.

The mood was also chilly in the hotel rooms where the Tigerbelles stayed in London. Jealous of her fame, some of Wilma's teammates acted cold and distant. Some stopped speaking to her. During a relay race in London, Wilma's three teammates actually held back, determined not to give Wilma Rudolph any more glory. They ran halfheartedly and left her with a 40-meter gap to close in the last leg. Angry at her teammates, Wilma pushed as hard as she could and won the race, by inches. Coach Temple saw it all and put everyone on the relay team on probation, meaning he would suspend any member who made more trouble.

London wasn't the end of the road. The team spent several more weeks in Europe, running and winning sprints and relays in several cities. Wherever she went, Wilma was met by large crowds of admirers. One fan in Berlin, Germany, even stole her track shoes.

Finally, the day came to pack up for the last time. Wilma flew to New York, then to Nashville, then got a ride the fifty miles back to Clarksville. She was finally going home, where a lot of people were waiting just for her.

Chapter | Eight

A Triumphant Return

Big crowds met Wilma when she returned to the United States. Photographers and newspaper reporters arrived at her home in Clarksville, wanting pictures and stories. Friends arrived to talk, and strangers asked for her autograph.

The city of Clarksville held the biggest parade in its history for a young woman from the poorest neighborhood in town. The line of cars and its police escort snaked past thousands of cheering people. Wilma's mother and father rode in the parade. Coach Gray was there, and so was two-year-old Yolanda. The parade included marching bands from the city's African American and white schools and army troops and officers from nearby Fort Campbell, Kentucky. In the lead was Wilma Rudolph, waving to the crowds from the backseat of a convertible.

For the first time in the history of Clarksville, whites and African Americans took part in a public event together. For one day at least, the old barriers of segregation came down. Everyone was just a proud citizen of Clarksville, cheering the city's hero.

SULLIVAN RUNNER-UP

Each year, the Amateur Athletic Union names the winner of the Sullivan Award. This award honors the best amateur athlete in the country. Wilma Rudolph was a strong candidate for the award in 1960, and the vote was close. At the final tally, she finished second, the only race she lost that year. She lost to a very worthy opponent, Rafer Johnson, an athlete from Texas who had won the Olympic decathlon, an event made up of ten different track-and-field contests.

That evening, the city held a banquet in Wilma's honor at the Clarksville Armory. It too was an integrated event. Wilma never forgot the words spoken that night by W. D. Hudson, a Montgomery County judge and the former mayor of Clarksville. In his speech, he looked out at the audience of black and white faces. He said, "Ladies and gentlemen, you play a piano. You can play very nice music on a piano by playing only the black keys on it, and you can play very nice music on the same piano by playing only the white keys on it. But ladies and gentlemen, the absolute best music comes out of that piano when you play both the black keys and the white keys together."

Wilma enjoyed the praise and fine words, but she had worries as well. Her father had developed a disease called diabetes. He was growing sicker. On the night of the Clarksville banquet, he even collapsed for a moment. But he told Wilma not to mind about him—he wanted her to enjoy the spotlight.

Wilma also worried about money. She wanted to keep her amateur (unpaid) status so she would be eligible to compete in another Olympics. That meant she couldn't run for prize money. Wilma wondered how she would support herself as an amateur athlete.

A few days after the Clarksville parade, another parade took place in Louisville, Kentucky. There, another young Olympic champion was treated like royalty. He was Cassius Clay, the outspoken young boxer whom Wilma had met in Rome. He too had won a gold medal.

Cassius invited Wilma to join his motorcade and to sit beside him in the car that carried him through town. As the parade went up Walnut Street in downtown Louisville, Cassius yelled out her name to the crowd. "And this . . . is Wilma Rudolph. She is the greatest. . . . Come on, Wilma, stand up!" Cassius's confidence and charisma electrified the crowds, but he couldn't persuade Wilma to stand up and share the spotlight.

She just sank down into her seat, timid and unhappy with the noisy crowds and the attention.

THE GREATEST

Boxer Cassius Clay, who like Wilma Rudolph rose to fame at the Rome Olympics, was brash and outspoken. He called himself the greatest and predicted that he would win every fight. After his victory in Rome, he wore his gold medal everywhere he went. In 1964 Clay became a member of the Nation of Islam, a controversial Muslim organization, and changed his name to Muhammad Ali. The same year, he won the heavyweight crown in professional boxing. He won the title again in 1974 and 1978.

After all the excitement, Wilma wanted a few days of rest. She had been all over Europe and back, but her traveling had just begun. Shortly after her return to Tennessee, Wilma prepared for a grand tour that the TSU Alumni Association had organized. A little touring group—including her mother, Coach Temple, and a few others, set out from Clarksville.

Their first stop was Chicago, where Mayor Richard Daley offered Wilma the keys to the city—meaning that Wilma was the most important guest in town. Then she visited Detroit,

Michigan; Atlanta, Georgia; and New York City, where Roy Wilkins, head of the National Association for the Advancement of Colored People (NAACP), gave a speech in her honor. Wilkins and the NAACP were leading the fight for civil rights—the fair and equal treatment of African American citizens in the United States. In Wilkins's view, Wilma's accomplishments at the Olympic Games showed that African Americans could overcome any obstacle, whether a physical disability or discrimination, to reach their goals.

Wilma's fancy nicknames, including the Black Gazelle and the Black Pearl, never caught on in the United States. There, she was always known by her old high school basketball nickname, Skeeter.

Wilma saw Philadelphia and then Washington, D.C., where she met ambassadors, senators, and someone she never expected to meet, no matter how many track events she won. A graduate of Tennessee State had arranged for Wilma to visit the White House and to meet President John F. Kennedy. Elected in November 1960, Kennedy had just begun serving his term of office. He had watched the Olympics on television and had admired Wilma's running. He wanted to shake her hand at the White House.

Wilma arrived at the White House feeling nervous, with her mother and Coach Temple beside her. Security agents escorted her through the building. In the Oval Office, where the president worked, Kennedy greeted her and invited her to sit down for a chat. He complimented her on her running and joked about the many different nicknames for Wilma that were appearing in the press. They talked for about half an hour. It was another highlight from a year of incredible moments, and a moment she wouldn't forget.

The tour went on for months. When she returned to Nashville and Tennessee State, Wilma tried to change back into an ordinary college student. She held a job in the university post office and joined a sorority—a club of female students who lived together in a big house. In the classroom, she majored in education. But returning to her old life wasn't easy. "You become world famous and you sit with kings and queens. . . . You can't go back to living the way you did before because you've been taken out of one setting and shown the other. That becomes a struggle and makes you struggle," Wilma remarked.

Wilma had to consider her future. The next Summer Olympics would take place in 1964. If she wanted to take part, she would have to train. She would have to work on her starts, of course, and consider which events were her strongest.

But going back to the Olympics presented one serious problem: Wilma would be competing against only herself. No other female runner from the 1960 Olympics had matched her accomplishments. No other American woman had ever won three gold medals. To better her performance in Rome, she would have to win more gold, and that meant preparing for new events. If she couldn't take the gold in every one, she knew, she would be remembered by some as a loser, a failure. "I could match my three gold medals, but I've already done that now," she said. "If I got two, instead of it being a thrill it would be a disappointment." Wilma's plans began to change. Instead of the 1964 Olympics, she started to think about retirement.

In February 1961, Wilma was invited to the famous Millrose Games at Madison Square Garden in New York City. The event had been founded in 1908 by Rodman Wanamaker, the son of a wealthy department store owner. It soon became the world's most prestigious track-and-field event. The showcase race of the Millrose Games had always been the one-mile race, called the Wanamaker Mile.

But in 1961, Wilma Rudolph was the showcase. She and a few other competitors became the first women to participate in the Millrose Games in thirty years. In the 60-yard sprint, she tied her own world record time of 6.9 seconds.

Two weeks later, Wilma and some of her competitors became the first female athletes to take part in the New York Athletic Club games at Madison Square Garden. At that event, Wilma beat her 60-yard mark by one-tenth of a second. Soon afterward, at a meet in Louisville, she set a new world record in the 70-yard sprint. She finished in 7.8 seconds, smashing the old record of 8.2 seconds.

LATE-NIGHT RACE

The famous Wanamaker Mile, the prestige event of the Millrose Games, is always run at 10:00 P.M. The tradition stems from the years before television, when radio sportscaster Ted Husing broadcast the race at ten in the evening, during the nightly news. In 2006 the ninety-ninth annual Millrose Games were held in New York City's Madison Square Garden.

Wilma also experienced sadness that year. Her father's health didn't improve, and in April 1961, he died. Ed Rudolph had been an example of strength and discipline in Wilma's life. He was especially proud of guiding and supporting his huge family through tough times.

The following year, in 1962, Wilma prepared for a special meet. A group of U.S. runners would compete against a team from the Soviet Union. The meet took place during the Cold War, a time of great hostility between the two countries. The Stanford track coach, Payton Jordan, arranged the meet with a Soviet sports official. More than 150,000 people attended the meet.

> ❝I wanted to retire with a winning attitude and on a winning note. My last race was in Palo Alto, California, Stanford University, 1962, the U.S.S.R. [Soviet Union] versus the United States. By that time, I had sat with kings and queens and prime ministers, you name it. How can you top that?❞
>
> —WILMA RUDOLPH

The meet was scheduled for July, at Stanford University in California. Coach Temple worked Wilma hard to prepare. By the time she got to Stanford, she was back in Olympic condition. Wilma had no trouble winning the 100-meter sprint. As the anchor for the relay team, she led the Americans to a victory over a very strong Soviet squad.

By then Wilma was set on retirement. But she wanted to go out in style, running in good form, winning, and standing at attention as the national anthem played. The victories at Stanford convinced her that the time had come to end her running career. The Stanford meet was the last she would participate in as a runner.

Chapter Nine

A New Track

After retiring from track, Wilma Rudolph wanted a normal life and a career that would challenge and interest her. But what could possibly match competing on the Olympic stage, winning gold medals, and hearing the roar of adoring crowds?

She faced a difficult decision and an uncertain future. In the 1960s, even the best female athletes had few options for a career in sports. Men who played baseball, football, or basketball could play in a professional league. But there was no organized league for track teams—male or female. Coaching was a possibility, and certainly Ed Temple would have found a position for Wilma as a Tigerbelles coach. But full-time coaching didn't interest her much. When she was at the track, she wanted to run, not stand on the sidelines.

The situation could make anyone feel strange and sometimes bitter. Here she was, a famous athlete, with her picture in newspapers all over the world, and her most serious problem was how to make a living! Wilma still enjoyed her athletic fame, and the U.S. government sent her on goodwill trips to Africa and Asia. There, to raise friendly feelings for the United States, she shook many hands and smiled for the cameras. But at home, Wilma didn't have a steady income. It wasn't common for companies to hire athletes to endorse products in those days. But even the companies that did hire athletes wouldn't hire African American women.

 In 2004 the U.S. Postal Service put Wilma's picture on a twenty-three-cent postage stamp.

Wilma would have liked to talk things over with Coach Gray, the man who had made her into a basketball player and an athlete. But in 1962, the Burt High coach died in a car accident. Robert broke the news, just as Wilma was getting ready for a trip to Asia. It was hard to realize that the man who had meant so much to her life was gone. Wilma couldn't bring herself to attend the funeral. Instead, she wrote a letter of farewell and had someone read it out loud at the funeral.

All the while, Wilma had her young daughter to care for. She would need more than fame to survive and raise a family. So she made sure to complete college. She received a bachelor's degree in education, graduating from TSU on May 27, 1963. After graduation, she finally returned to Clarksville. Back at her mother's home, she had the chance to think about the future.

> 66 *She has always been my number one hero. She was in a class by herself, to have such excellence in athletics, to have the strength to overcome polio and to be a great leader. I don't think the footprints that Wilma laid could ever be filled.* 99
>
> —TRACK-AND-FIELD GOLD MEDALIST JACKIE JOYNER-KERSEE

Wilma also married her high school sweetheart, Robert Eldridge, who was still a college student. Because so many people wanted to come to her wedding, she held the ceremony in a big open field, decorated with an altar and hundreds of blue flowers. That evening guests attended receptions at Blanche Rudolph's home and the American Legion Hall in Clarksville. Soon afterward, Wilma learned that she was expecting another baby.

Wilma visited Cobb Elementary, her old school, and remembered the good times she had enjoyed as a student there.

With her degree in education, she was qualified for a teaching job. She applied and was accepted as a second-grade teacher at her former school. In her eyes, teaching a second-grade class was a way of guiding young people and making a contribution to their lives. She had gone through a tough physical challenge when she was the age of her students, which made her sympathetic to their problems.

---

66 When the sun is shining I can do anything; no mountain is too high, no trouble too difficult. 99

—WILMA RUDOLPH

Wilma wanted to bring new, creative ideas into the classroom, but these ideas didn't spark much interest among her fellow teachers or the principal. She was told to teach as usual, from the books assigned to her class. Very soon she was feeling frustrated. In addition, the low salary she earned barely supported her and her family. And that family was growing. In May 1964, Wilma gave birth to her second daughter, Djuana.

In the fall of 1964, Wilma returned to Cobb Elementary for another year of teaching. By the end of the school year, she was expecting her third child, Robert Jr., and giving serious thought to a change. She had an offer to move to Evansville, Indiana, and to manage a community center. In the summer of 1965, she accepted the job. She and her family left Clarksville.

Wilma was suited to her job in Evansville. She was a good organizer, and she enjoyed planning special events and athletic programs. But she knew there were better opportunities in other places, perhaps in other countries. That year, she wrote a letter to the Job Corps, a U.S. government agency that helped poor people train for and find new employment.

A Job Corps director, Frank Bispham, invited her to Boston for an interview. Of course, Bispham and everyone else knew who Wilma Rudolph was. Simply as a star athlete, she would attract people to the organization and help it thrive. The Job Corps invited Wilma to join its program in Poland Spring, a resort area in Maine. It was a relatively small program, but it would help her gain experience.

In Poland Spring, Wilma served as director of a girls physical education program. She led practices and coached track and basketball teams. She also gave advice on life and work to the girls taking part.

In 1967 she received a letter and invitation from Vice President Hubert Humphrey. He wanted her to take a short-term job with Operation Champion. This U.S. government program worked with talented young athletes in several big cities. It ran programs in track, football, basketball, and swimming. Wilma would help with girls' track, traveling from one city to the next to train runners and set up competitions.

As a member of Operation Champion, Wilma traveled all over the country, opening sports clinics and facilities and consulting with university track teams. After completing her assignment, she returned to her work with the Job Corps. But she asked for a transfer from Poland Spring to someplace closer to her hometown. The Job Corps moved her from Maine to Saint Louis, Missouri.

When her sister Charlene, who lived in Detroit, came down with a serious illness, Wilma and the family moved again. They settled in Detroit so Wilma could help her sister. She took a teaching position at Pelham Junior High School.

The many moves didn't cure Wilma's feelings of frustration and aimlessness. In the spring of 1968, she and the family left Detroit and returned to Clarksville. She wasn't sure where to go, or when to go, or whether she should just stay home and live out her life in the town where she had grown up. She began to feel depressed.

Seeking advice, she made a call to Bill Russell, a basketball player for the Boston Celtics whom she had met after the 1956 Olympics. Russell had dealt with many of the same frustrations—although as a basketball player, he was able to make a living playing the sport he loved.

He suggested a complete change: California. Although Russell had played for the Celtics since 1956, he had grown up in the San Francisco Bay Area, in northern California. Wilma was soon packing her bags for Los Angeles, in southern California.

Wilma took a job in Watts, a poor, mostly African American area of Los Angeles. A few years before, the neighborhood had erupted in violence, as crowds of African Americans took to the streets out of frustration with poverty, unemployment, and police brutality. Arsonists burned hundreds of buildings, and many people died in the rioting.

LIFE STORIES

In 1975 Wilma's story inspired a NBC television movie, *Wilma*, starring Shirley Jo Finney as Wilma and Cicely Tyson as Blanche Rudolph. The role of Robert Eldridge, Wilma's boyfriend and then husband, provided the debut for a young actor who would go on to bigger, better roles and Hollywood stardom. His name was Denzel Washington. Wilma published her autobiography, *Wilma: The Story of Wilma Rudolph*, in 1977.

Wilma worked with the Watts Community Action Committee, which was trying to rebuild the community after the riots. Like the Job Corps, the committee was a service organization dedicated to helping young people and poor people improve their lives. Later, Rudolph accepted a position with the University of California at Los Angeles (UCLA), where she worked as an administrator in the Afro-American studies program. In 1971 she gave birth to her fourth child, a son named Xurry.

HONORING WILMA RUDOLPH

Wilma Rudolph received many honors in her lifetime. Some of the most meaningful came from her hometown and home state. For instance, the city of Clarksville recognized Wilma Rudolph as one of its most famous natives. The city named an important street Wilma Rudolph Boulevard and raised a bronze statue of Wilma at the corner of College Street and Riverside Drive. On December 2, 1980, Tennessee State University named its indoor track after her.

Although her work was enjoyable, Wilma soon found herself feeling restless again. In addition, she and Robert had been growing apart. In 1976 the couple divorced. Wilma found herself a single mother of four, still struggling to pay her bills and to find challenge and fulfillment in her work.

She seemed to have a difficult time staying in one place. She kept moving and changing her scene as quickly as possible.

She left Los Angeles for Chicago, then moved to Charleston, West Virginia, where she helped raise money for a track-and-field Hall of Fame. Then she returned to Clarksville again. Along the way, she won several awards for her achievements. She was elected to the Black Sports Hall of Fame in 1980.

In 1982 Wilma moved with her children to Indianapolis, Indiana. There she founded the Wilma Rudolph Foundation, a group dedicated to organizing community track-and-field teams. Wilma remained in Indianapolis for ten years, finally finding a career and a place she could settle into. She still made speeches, and she became a spokeswoman for some large food companies. In 1984 she attended a special ceremony at the U.S. Olympic Hall of Fame, where she was inducted as a member.

In addition to her work with her foundation, Wilma coached track at DePauw University, not far from Indianapolis. She also worked as a radio talk-show host. She joined the boards of directors of banks and other companies. In 1992 she became the vice president of Baptist Hospital in Nashville. She still spent a lot of time on the road, traveling to meetings and public events. In June 1993, Wilma, golfer Arnold Palmer, basketball pro Kareem Abdul-Jabbar, boxer Muhammad Ali (the former Cassius Clay), and baseball star Ted Williams were honored by President Bill Clinton as the "Great Ones" at the first National Sports Awards.

But Wilma's problems continued. She never achieved financial independence. Even as she won awards and recognition, she tangled with the Internal Revenue Service over taxes she owed to the U.S. government. In early 1994, her mother died. Shortly afterward Wilma herself fell seriously ill. After giving a speech in Atlanta, she was diagnosed with brain cancer.

Wilma had overcome many difficulties in her life. She was sure she would overcome cancer as well. But the cancer treatments made her feel even sicker. Despite the best efforts of her doctors, the cancer spread. Wilma stopped making public appearances. To keep up her spirits, she joined Coach Temple for walks around the campus and running track at Tennessee State.

Just a few months after she was diagnosed with cancer, on November 12, 1994, Wilma Rudolph died in Nashville, Tennessee. She was only fifty-four years old.

 In the days after Wilma's death in 1994, flags all over Tennessee flew at half-mast.

Thousands of people packed Kean Hall at TSU for a memorial service. Shortly afterward friends and family gathered for a funeral at the First Baptist Church in Clarksville. There, four decades earlier, Wilma had walked down the aisle without a leg brace and won her first important triumph, over polio. The state of Tennessee honored Wilma in 1997 by naming June 23, the date of her birth, as Wilma Rudolph Day.

Epilogue

Struggle and Triumph

Wilma Rudolph always searched for challenge. She faced it very early in life, when polio struck and she couldn't even walk. She overcame this challenge with many years of hard work. She then set an even bigger goal, to become the fastest woman on earth. For a time in 1960, she attained her goal and the honors that came with it. For the rest of her life, she searched for more challenges and strove to overcome the barriers she faced as a woman and as an African American.

Along the way, Wilma became an inspiration to the next generation of track stars. Florence Griffith Joyner, who won three gold medals at the 1988 Summer Olympics in Seoul, South Korea; Jackie Joyner-Kersee, a gold-medal-winning long jumper and heptathlete; and many others looked up to Wilma. They all tried to match her accomplishments and to learn from her Olympic example.

In the 1980s, Wilma and Joyner-Kersee became close friends. "She was always in my corner. . . . If I had a problem, I could call her at home. It was like talking to someone you knew for a lifetime," Jackie remembers. Florence Griffith Joyner (who was also Jackie's sister-in-law) added, "Whenever· I was down . . . I often thought how dedicated Wilma was to overcome the obstacles. That motivates me to push harder."

Florence Griffith Joyner—nicknamed FloJo—set the world record for women in the 100-meter sprint in 1998. That year at a track in Indianapolis, Indiana, she ran the distance in 10.49 seconds. At the Olympic Games later that year, FloJo set a record in the finals of the 200-meter sprint, with a time of 21.34 seconds. The most remarkable thing about these records is that as of early 2006—more than ten years after FloJo set them—no woman had recorded a better time in either event.

But Wilma Rudolph wasn't just an inspiration to professional athletes. She was a role model for all girls. She reflected: "The triumph can't be had without the struggle. And I know what struggle is. I have spent a lifetime trying to share what it has meant to be a woman first in the world of sports so that other young women have a chance to reach their dreams." At the National Sports Awards ceremony in 1993, President Bill Clinton said, "She broke barriers for thousands of women competitors and paved the way for those who have followed in her footsteps."

Wilma knew that for any runner, training is tough, both mentally and physically, and winning is impossible without total dedication. For her, as for other champion athletes, this hard work and dedication just came naturally.

PERSONAL STATISTICS

Name:

Wilma Glodean Rudolph

Nickname:

Skeeter, the Black Pearl, the Black Gazelle

Born:

June 23, 1940

Died:

November 12, 1994

Height:

5'11"

Weight:

130 lbs.

CAREER STATISTICS

1956 Summer Olympics (Melbourne)

    4x100-meter relay: 44.9 seconds (bronze medal)

1960 Summer Olympics (Rome)

    100-meter sprint: 11.0 seconds (gold medal)

    200-meter sprint: 24.0 seconds (gold medal)

    4x100-meter relay: 44.5 seconds (gold medal)

U.S. Track and Field Championships

    1959: 100-meter sprint (12.1 seconds)

    1960: 100-meter sprint (11.5 seconds)

    1960: 200-meter sprint (22.9 seconds)

    1961: 100-yard sprint (10.8 seconds)

GLOSSARY

amateur: an athlete who earns no money from competition

baton: a cylinder of aluminum or wood, passed by runners during a relay race

disability: a physical or mental impairment

heat: one of several preliminary races, held to determine the athletes for final competition

integration: the mixing of people of different races at schools, restaurants, and other public places

poliomyelitis: a viral disease that can cause permanent damage to the victim's arms, legs, or other parts of the body

scholarship: an award of money given to a student to help pay for his or her education

segregation: the separation of people of different races at schools, restaurants, and other public places

sprint: a short-distance footrace

starting block: a device that supports a sprinter's back foot at the starting line

BIBLIOGRAPHY

Fischer, David. *The Encyclopedia of the Summer Olympics.* New York: Franklin Watts, 2003.

Haley, Alex. "The Queen Who Earned Her Crown." In *The Unlevel Playing Field: A Documentary History of the African American Experience in Sport*, edited by David K. Wiggins and Patrick B. Miller, pp. 263–68. Urbana: University of Illinois Press, 2005.

Libby, Bill. *Stars of the Olympics.* New York: Hawthorn Books, 1975.

McElroy, Kathleen. "Somewhere to Run." In *Nike Is a Goddess: The History of Women in Sports*, edited by Lissa Smith, pp. 3–30. Boston: Atlantic Monthly Press, 1988.

Rudolph, Wilma. *Wilma: The Story of Wilma Rudolph.* New York: New American Library, 1977.

Sears, Edward S. *Running Through the Ages.* Jefferson, NC: McFarland & Company, 2001.

Tricard, Louise M. *American Women's Track and Field: A History, 1895 through 1980.* Jefferson, NC: McFarland & Company, 1996.

WEB SITES

Black History—Biography

http://www.galegroup.com/free_resources/bhm/bio/rudolph_w.htm

This site offers a biography of Wilma Rudolph as part of the Black History series.

National Women's Hall of Fame—Women of the Hall

http://www.greatwomen.org/women.php?action=viewone&id=131

Here, the National Women's Hall of Fame offers a biography of Wilma Rudolph, along with quick facts and a list of resources.

Wilma Rudolph Quotes

http://womenshistory.about.com/od/quotes/a/wilma_rudolph.htm

This Web page offers a collection of quotes from Wilma Rudolph about her life and her track career.

INDEX